D1384205

EP *to* LU

EP to LU

NINE LETTERS WRITTEN
TO LOUIS UNTERMEYER BY

Ezra Pound

EDITED BY J. A. ROBBINS

Indiana University Press / 1963
Bloomington

ACKNOWLEDGMENTS

I AM indebted to Mr. Pound for permission to publish the letters; to Mr. Untermeyer for his interest and assistance; to Mr. Robert M. MacGregor of New Directions; to Mr. Herbert P. Gleason; to Mr. Harry M. Meacham; to Professor Norman Holmes Pearson; to Mr. Donald C. Gallup; to Mr. John Cournos; and to Mr. James Rader, a graduate of Wabash College who has explored Pound's brief stay there.

The verse quoted in the note to Letter VI is from *Heinrich Heine, Paradox and Poet: The Poems,* by Louis Untermeyer, copyright 1937 by Harcourt, Brace & World, Inc. and reprinted with their permission.

J. A. R.

———

THE partial reproductions of three of the letters will give the reader some sense of Pound's early hand and typing style. The signature which appears on the title page comes from Letter I.

———

CONTENTS

INTRODUCTION   7

THE LETTERS

I	London, January 8, 1914	11
II	Rapallo, December 30, 1929	12
III	Rapallo, January 2, 1930	13
IV	Rapallo, early 1930	14
V	Rapallo, early 1930	15
VI	Rapallo, March 1, 1930	20
VII	Rapallo, March 19, 1930	25
VIII	Venice, June 26, 1930	26
IX	Rapallo, July 13, 1931	27

NOTES   29

WORKS CITED   47

A NOTE ON THE EDITING

ANYONE familiar with Ezra Pound's typed letters knows that he long ago subdued the typewriter to his personality. His typing "style" is instantly recognizable, with the unique use of capitals, spacing, indentation, slant marks, and periods—as well as abbreviations (such as the familiar *wd.* for *would*), pejorative spellings (such as *publik*), and unique punctuation (such as *e;g;*). I have followed the precedent of D. D. Paige in his *Letters of Ezra Pound* and have regularized the typed manuscripts by paragraphing and occasionally by adding punctuation, as an aid to the reader. Misspellings have been allowed to stand, un-*sic*-ed, though a few typing errors have been silently corrected. Holograph additions not inserted by caret, arrow, or line are here printed where they occur in the manuscript. In essence these letters have been altered minimally and only when readability seemed to require it.

The editor is aware that not all of the annotation will be of interest to the knowledgeable, but he has hoped, rather, to supply such commentary as will make the volume meaningful to anyone who may look into it.

INTRODUCTION

THE poetry of our century in the English language would be a far different thing but for three men whose paths and minds and art came together in rare conjunction in London some five decades ago. The three—Yeats from Ireland, Eliot and Pound from America—gave to twentieth-century poetry a twentieth-century voice which, nonetheless, reflected the richness of the past. In unique ways each helped to make this unpoetic century resound with fresh and powerful cadence.

For a time London was the capital of modern poetry and, in the case of the two younger Americans, their careers as poets virtually commenced in that city. From that time onward—the year was 1908—Pound began his restless and probing life as poet, ranging through letters and the other arts as though they were his private province. He was both theoretician and practitioner, both strategist and captain of the barricades. With an apostolic sense of mission, by example and pronouncement, Pound cherished and championed all in life and art that seemed vital and immediate to him, whether of his age or of the past.

Of the three poets, Pound was the most energetic—and the noisiest. He never shirked any contest or undertook any cause with timidity. If he tended to overargue and berate, it was because he felt and cared deeply. "Excitement," M. L. Rosenthal recently said, "attends almost all of Ezra Pound's prose and poetry—the excitement of the man himself, his urgency and cantankerousness and virtuosity. Also, he has *authority*. In part this is the irritating authority of the self-appointed leader, yet it is indisputable." Self appointed he was indeed, yet he could have been impeached or passed by. He was not. He touched the lives of scores of artists, often at a time of artistic or personal need. He had an uncanny instinct in seeking out the best new writers, and he aided them artistically and materially, often when help was most wanted. His encouragement of James Joyce at a dark moment of his career is a striking instance of Pound's artistic paternalism, all the more notable because Joyce was yet to do his greatest work and because the two had yet to meet. Pound's letters are so filled with Pound that we risk forgetting his capacity for selflessness simply because he was uncharacteristically so modest where help to others was concerned.

The letters to Louis Untermeyer here printed are a minor segment of his great epistolary outpouring—so voluminous that they form a second career, but these letters and notes to Untermeyer are alive with the energies, concerns, and dogmatisms of the man. The longest and most significant of these is a five-page biographical summary, which Pound presented to Untermeyer in Rapallo in 1930. It bears the inscription, in Untermeyer's hand, "Ezra Pound to LU—a statement 'in order to put the facts straight',", and it came to Untermeyer when he was preparing a new edition of his *Modern American Poetry*. In the first edition of this famous anthology in 1919 Untermeyer had printed three of Pound's poems. Two were added in the second edition (1921); and in the more ambitious third edition (1925) Untermeyer had added biographical and critical headnotes for all the poets and had increased the number of Pound's poems to eight. Just prior to the fourth edition (1930), Untermeyer and his wife visited Pound in Rapallo. The talk turned to anthologies and, hoping for certain changes in the new edition,

Pound sat down at his typewriter to reduce his life and career to five illuminating pages. In the new volume, without pulling his critical punches (two of Pound's early volumes, he said, "contain the germs of dessication and decay"), Untermeyer faithfully incorporated information which Pound had supplied, including mention of Pound's invention of the term "imagism," his priority in introducing Oriental poetry and in recognizing Tagore and Joyce, his being without honor in his own country, and the general "coherent design" of his work. The other letters range widely in subject—literature and art in 1914 London, the hotels in Rapallo, Fenollosa's manuscripts on Oriental drama and poetry, translating Heine, Sicilian donkeys, American publishers, and the making of anthologies.

Mr. Untermeyer, who has known the poets of this century both personally and professionally, recently deposited his poetry collection in the Lilly Library of Indiana University. Accompanying the first editions of Pound's works were these letters, written between 1914 and 1933. They have been kept together over the years and deserve here to be printed together.

J. A. ROBBINS

10 Church Walk, Kensington
London. W

Dear Louis Untermeyer:

I find yr. note in my desk & as it isn't marked answered, I conclude I never did answer it or send you "Ripostes" which is now too late for review—but I wasn't sending it especially for review in any case.

No. "Poetry" isn't entirely glorious. I've resigned once as a protest against the rot they put in, & I've gone back in the vain hope of keeping it from getting worse.

Still I think their intention is moderately good.

I've been living with Yeats in the country for the past 2 months.

Cournos & I have found a very powerful young sculptor, Gaudier Brzeska.

I've come in for Fenollosa's very valuable *mss.* on the Japanese "Noh" plays & the Chinese Lyric. I suppose I'll have the first paper on same in the "Quarterly Review" for about May.

I should think that was about my news.

The Glebe is bringing out an Imagiste anthology in February (I think).

I should have some hopes of a new paper here, The Egoist, if I had sufficient financial backing.

Cournos has done a "History of American painting."

He is probably going to N. Y. for a visit shortly.

Send on yr. vol. s. v. p.

Yours sincerely

8.1.14   EZRA POUND

Rapallo
Via Marsala, 12 Int. 5
30 Dec. [*1929*]

Dear Untermeyer.

Buon anno.

Yes, am in residence. Shdnt. think you need reserve rooms. The hotels will prob. fill up a bit after new years but no sign of crowding yet. You dont ask for advice regarding the caravansaries so I refrain from giving any.

yrs.
E P

Rapallo
Via Marsala, 12 Int. 5
2 jan [1930]

Dear L. U.

The Casino is better at twice the price, cant be done on licherchoor alone, but if you are representing the family banking house, by all means dont deprive etc. . .

The Europa is, I think the worst placed hotel in Rap. Savoia much better (I usually send comfortable bourgeois there, cook not so good this year as two years ago). The Moderno was good enough for Vail-Guggenheims. (No reports on present cuisine available.)

There are others at a few lire less per diem.

Bristol *has* an aussicht and also the Verdi if you want to study english pathology. both comfortable. (save for mentality of the denizens.)

On the hole shd. suggest Savoia or Moderno. unless you want eyetalyan ammosphere. in which case the Marsala and Rosa Bianca are both on the sea front. but lack drawrin rooms. However; licherary gents have survived 'em and a front room in the Marsala gets all the sun there is.

                    E P

Zallamarr o price. Town accomodates at from 23 to 123 per diem. and nobody cares a damn which anyone else uses. There is no populace to be impressed.

Rapallo
Via Marsala, 12 Int. 5
[Early 1930]

I will be pleased to dine on Friday—
shall not dress unless special request or
ukase to that effect is recd.

Yrs

E. P.

[Rapallo, 1930]

Entered U. P. Penn at 15 with intention of studying comparative values in literature (poetry) and began doing so unbeknown to the faculty. 1902 enrolled as special student to avoid irrelevant subjects. 1903-5 continued process at Hamilton College under W. P. Shepard, "Schnitz" Brant and J. D. Ibbotson. 1905-07 P. G. at U. of Penn. Chiefly impressed by lack of correlation between different depts. and lack either of general survey of literature or any coherent interest in literature as such (as distinct for example from philology). 07-08 Instructor with Professorial functions at Wabash College, Crawfordsville, Ind., the "Athens of the West", a town with literary traditions "Lew Wallace died there." E. P. was fired at the end of 4 months, all accusations save that of his being "the latin Quarter type" having been ultimately refuted. But the widow never married the President of the College after all.

1908 landed in Gibralter with 80 dollar and lived on the interest for some time. Life saved by Yusuf Benamore. (tourists please note and use the Benamore family if couriers are required.)

1908 A Lume Spento printed in Venice. Quinzaine, London.

1909: Personae (spring), Exultations (Autumn), quoted (with expurgations) in the International Sunday School lessons. etc. after which his intellexshul biography is largely contained in his publications (vide English Who's Who, E. P. having been expurgated from the American Who's Who for disorderly conduct).

In 1912 invented terms "Imagiste" and Imagisme,

Ezra Pound to Ill - a Statement
"in order to put the facts straight."
Rapallo. 1932.

Entererd U.P. Penn at 15 with intention of studying
comparative values in literature (poetry) and began
doing so unbeknown to the faculty. 1902 enrolled
as special student to avoid irrelevant subjects. 1903=5
continued process at Hamilton College under W.P.Shepard
,"Schmitz" Brandt and J.D.Ibbotsen. 1905=07 P.G. at U. of
Penn. 07=08 Instructor with Professorial functions at
Wabash College Crawfordsville Ind. the " Athens of the
West " , a town with literary traditions " Lew Wallace
died there." E.P. was fired at the end of 4 months
all accusations save that of his being " the latin Quarter
type " having been ultimately refuted. But the widow
never married the President of the College after all.

(1908)
~~Penn~~ landed in Gibralter with 80 dollar and
lived on the interest for some time. Life saved by
Yusuf Benamore. (tourists please note and use the
Benamore family if couriers are required.)

1908   A Lume Spento printed in Venice. Quinzaine , London.
1909 : Persenae (spring) Exultations (Autumn) , quoted &
(with expurgations) in the International Sunday School
lessons. etc. after WH which his intellexshul biography
                                        (English)
is largely contained in his publications (vide Who's Who
E.P. having been expurgated from the American Who's Who
for disorderly conduct.

                                  (the latter)
In 1912 invented terms " Imagiste " and Imagisme, in order
to avoid vain gabble as to the nature of poetry . Has
no objection to pleasure others have had in exploiting
these lables and offering cheap imitation , but
regrets loss of critical distinction between
poetry which

the latter in order to avoid vain gabble as to the nature of poetry. Has no objection to pleasure others have had in exploiting these labels and offering cheap imitation, but regrets loss of critical distinction between poetry which "uses no word which does not contribute to the presentation" and verbosity (more or less rhythmic). Had no connection with the Amygist movement in American verse.

Invented the term vorticism and contributed to Wyndham Lewis "Blast" in 1914.

1927 produced "How to Read," summary of his critical conclusions, exposition of a method and proof that his various prose books and literary studies had not been hap hazard dilletantism but done in pursuance with plan and coherent design.

1910-29 examination of neglected sections of society (i.e. sections neglected by uplift societies, Paul Morand, labour, etc.)

1917-20 study of musicians on the hoof. 1919-21 composed an opera "Le Testament" (words by François Villon, plot and music by E. P.) opera edited by G. Antheil 1924.

Books still in print. *Personae* (the collected poems, save the Cantos, Liveright 1926, 2nd. edtn. 1927. Cantos I to XVI. Three Mts. Press, Paris 1925. Cantos XVII-XXVII, John Rodker, London 1927.

Books announced for 1930: Cantos I to XXX, Hours Press, Paris. The Poems of Guido Cavalcanti, definitive variorum text printed, edited by E. P. complete translation, with commentary and second complete text in Manul reproductions of mss. chosen so as to give full paleographic history of the poems. Aquila

Press, London. Collected Prose Work (folio) Aquila if the press survives the strain.

Collaboration with various reviews notably Poetry (1912-14), Little Review, Egoist 1913-15 (foreign edtr. 1917-19, introducing J. J's Ulysses, work of Eliot, Wynd. Lewis, etc.) Dial about 1920-21. Contributor to New Age 1912-20. Edtr. The Exile, 1927-28.

Social seat. London 1908-20. Paris 20-24. Rapallo 24–

////

Any attempt to do justice to P. shd. take count of the chronology of his work in relation to that by others. e. g. compare translations from the Chinese pubd. before his CATHAY (1915) and those published after that date.

The extent or "secret of his mysterious" influence can be gauged by comparing his critical action with that of the other "critics" who establish a reputation or position by safe rehash [of] what has already been said about accepted writers (of the past or present).

> When possible put
> DATES on poems.

Note his instant placing of authors now famous, e. g. the essay on Tagore (as literary artist not as messiah) that appeared in the Fortnightly immediately on pub. of Gitanjali.

The evaluation of Ulysses in the Mercure de France (June 1922) the first french critique of Joyce; establishing the proportion between Joyce and Flaubert.

Note also early essays of Joyce, Wyndham Lewis, etc; in 1913, 1914; cf. Pound essay on Eliot in 1917 with Edmund Wilson on Eliot in 1930.

Note also the several dozen well known authors poets and prosewriters who owe their first appearance in print or in america to P's intervention.

Quality to be judged progressive by the groupings of authors in the various reviews to which he has been official or unofficial advisor from the Egoist days onward. . .

Yet in 1930 P was able to state that NO american pubshr. had *ever* accepted a book on his recommendation! No am. univ. or cultural institution had ever invited him to lecture (this despite his double qualification as author and man of learning) nor had he ever been invited to serve on any jury of awards to art, music or literature, nor had any fellowship to a writer ever been made on his recommendation.

Not a complaint but an observation helping one calculate the state of intelligence in certain quarters.

By 1920 he had been excluded from every review or weekly Paper in England except the New Age.

The old magazines Harper Cent. Scrib. he has always regarded as a form of detritus; and the persistence with which they continue to reject the real thing when made and take the 3d rate immitation five ten twenty years later has never indicated a revision of his opinion.

Question of the accuracy or inaccuracy of P's scholarship can be best settled by someone who has tried to find an error in his life of S. Malatesta in the cantos, or in his edtn. of Cavalcanti.

Rapallo
Via Marsala, 12 Int. 5
1 Marzo [*1930*]

Dear Louis

Thanks for the two vols. and for prompt axshun re/
Harcourt's young.

The Heine, judged by any standard extant before I
so kussedly set up a ten bar fence is a capolavoro. And
there must be at least 50 of those I have already recd.
that get by even my barricade. Best, I think where you
have attempted most.

You have come so near a complete H. I think you
better finish the job. I might offer to help you fill in
lacunae; but you don't need any help. Neither I think
wd. it be worth bothering with anything but the meaning. Where the poems have been set to music you are
right to keep every syllable (I hope the b— y singers
are duly grateful); but for those that remain I don't
see that there is much point in bothering about it.
ANY tightening up of phrase being worth any possible
preservation of jingle.

I see with sorrow, or rather I dont see Diese Damen.
Lack of which (at least it isnt in yr. index and I haven't
found it in the book) lack of which has prompted the
following outrage which will, I hope, stir you into
making a better one.

These good ladies understand the
Honouring of poets, evergreen, Yes.

I Marze ⌐19 30⌐

①

Dear Louis

Thnaks for the two vols. and for prompt axshun
re/ Harcourt's young.

The Heine , judged by any standard extant
before I se kussedly set up a ten bar fence is a
capolavero. And there must be at least 50 that get by
even my barricade. Best , I think where you have attempted
most.

You have come so near a complete H. I thin|< you
better finish the job , . I might offer to help you
fill in lacunae ; but you dont need any help. Neither I
think wd. it be worth bothering with anything but the
meaning. Where the poems have been set to music you
~~XXXXXHXXXXXXXXHH~~ are right to keep every syllable ; but
for these that remain I dont see that there is much
point in bothering about it ~~for them it.~~ ANY tightening
up of phrase being worth any possible preservation of
jingle.

I see with serrow , or rather I dont see Diese Damen.
Lack of which (at least it isnt in yr. index and I havent
found it in the book) lack of which has prompted
the following outrage which will , I hope , stir you into
making a better one.

These good ladies understand the
  Honouring of poets , evergreen, Yes ,
They have conferred a luncheon on
  Me and my genius.

The soup was superserumptuous   (or any other damn
                                          adjective)

The wine made all my senses burn ;
The fewl was wing'd , divine ,
  The hare done to a turn .

    Our talk, I think, turned on the art of verse
    ~~and from hunger and thirst relieved~~
    I thanked them for the ~~BSFUY~~ honour
      That I thus from them received.

and when my hunger was relieved

I have putt the cart before the horse shoving the conferred
up into line 3, etc.   however theu knowest ..... et ...

I think I've only one stricture to make on the translations
 and that is on the places where you call a persone a
 " one " (with adjective ; at end of line). I knew the
temptation ; and do NOT believe it is necessary to cede.

I suppose if you *did* complete the job , do a " Whole
Heine " and if you shd. then make a small book containing
only the ones you were content with ; that book wd. simply
stay in the shop. such is human kussedness. The IXXXIXXIX
Inted. exeellent.

The parodies almost too mild to be called parodies.
As studies in manner , yes.   and very good expesition
of the relative value of the dif. styles. The Browning making
very good poem for most of its length . The Walt.
is parody and damn good.

They have conferred a luncheon on
    Me and my genius.

The soup was superscrumptuous   (or any other
                                  damn adjective)
    The wine made all my senses burn;
The fowl was wing'd, divine,
    The hare done to a turn.

Our talk, I think, turned on the art of verse
    And when my hunger was relieved
I thanked them for the honour
    That I thus from them received.

I have putt the cart before the horse shoving the conferred up into line 3. etc. However thou knowest . . . . .
etc . . .

    I think I've only one stricture to make on the trans-
lations and that is on the places where you call a persone a "one" (with adjective; at end of line). I know
the temptation; and do NOT believe it is necessary to
cede.

    I suppose if you did complete the job, do a "Whole
Heine" and if you shd. then make a small book containing only the ones you were content with; that book
wd. simply stay in the shop. Such is human kussedness.
The Intod. excellent.

    The parodies almost too mild to be called parodies.

    [In line 10 of the poem, Pound has deleted, "And from hun-
ger and thirst relieved," and substituted the line as given above.]

As studies in manner, yes. And very good exposition of the relative value of the dif. styles. The Browning making very good poem for most of its length. The Walt. is parody and damn good. The other horace not in this discussion. Leave it till later.

Mr. Van D. certainly an ass in his selection from the Heine. He has taken NONE of the best.

As it is 7 years since you did the second edtn. Heine; I think a new swat wd. prob. complete the job.

und so weiter. Salut a madame.

ever
E. P.

Hope Cantos arrive some time.

Rapallo
Via Marsala, 12 Int. 5
19 March [1930]

Dear Louis

Recd. a proposition from Harcourt this a. m. Thank you. The bizniz side of the question will have to go via Curtis Brown. I dont know their N. Y. man (E. G. Rich) personally, but I dont think he will be unreasonable. Their London office saves me a good deal of bother.

Regards to J. S. U.

ever

E.

779 Zattere, Venice
some time in June   *[June 26, 1930]*

Damn Louis I told you I thought that Who Who's of saints had been done. (Vide verso.)

Harcourt contract had a joker in it (Bradley or Judas Isc?). However it was on a minor point. I hope to get it straightened out. I have agreed to main points, rate 4% etc. Thanks again for yr. intervention.

How's the Sicilian donkeys thrivin in the wilds of N. Y.

Best wishes.

Ever
E. POUND

Rapallo
Via Marsala, 12 Int. 5
13 July [*1931*]

Dear Untermeyer:

For the poems you mention the negotion shd/ go via Liveright, and the fee will have to be the regular 25 bucks each.

Harcourt sent me a contract with a clause in it which if not intended for fraud was certainly admirably designed to permit the pubshr/ to swindle the author.

Upon my detection of which they dropped the question of prose book. Which things being so I don't see that I can be expected to make concessions of the few cents I shd/ receive from ANY bk/ to be pubd/ by them.

As for "what wd. I suggest". What the hell is the use of yr/ asking such a question? You know perfectly well that the poems you have chosen are NOT those that I wd. have selected as illustrative.

I can't believe that you have any serious intention of wanting to convey my pt/ of view.

Prob/ those poems as suitable to the anthology publik etc. etc. etc. . . . .

Better leave it as a matter of business.

yrs/
E. P.

Greetings to Madame

NOTES

I

The Ripostes of Ezra Pound was first published in London in 1912 and in Boston the following year.

When Harriet Monroe circularized the younger poets in mid-1912 about her projected new magazine, *Poetry,* she received a long reply from Pound in which he offered his services and, she says, "I sent Pound an enthusiastic answer, asking him to represent *Poetry* abroad as Foreign Correspondent." [Monroe, 251.]* He promptly accepted and there followed a continuous stream of newsy letters, reviews, instructions, demands, and poems by himself and others. By March of the following year he was objecting to her strictures about some lines touching upon harlots and lusts. He felt that he did not really have *carte blanche* and there were differences over his friend Hueffer. He told Amy Lowell on November 26, 1913, "I've resigned from *Poetry* . . . I don't know yet whether I'm shed of the bloomin' paper or not"; and in early December wrote flatly to Miss Monroe, "if I stay on the magazine it has got to improve. . . . I will not have my name associated with it unless it does improve." [Paige, 26-27.] But Pound did continue as agent and adviser until 1916 and he kept in touch with the magazine until the thirties.

Yeats and Pound had met in 1909. The two soon-to-be-married bachelors had left London in November to spend

* References, here reduced to author and page, are given more fully on pages 47-48.

a few weeks in Sussex, a sojourn which Pound described as "placid."

John Cournos, born in Kiev in 1881, was brought to America at the age of ten; but, dissatisfied with his routine life, he went to England at the age of thirty-one and published his first novel at thirty-eight. Cournos and his English wife were living in England at this time, 1914.

Henri Gaudier-Brzeska, the French sculptor born in 1891, was at this time working in London. He had held the first exhibition of his work the year before, in 1913. Pound and Cournos tell differing stories of how they met the artist. According to Pound, he and a friend attended an art show in search of new work and, as they paused before Gaudier-Brzeska's, Pound began word play with the consonantal peculiarities of his name. The artist, who had come up behind them, pronounced it correctly, "with the gentlest fury in the world," and disappeared. Pound wrote, inviting him to dinner, and thus the friendship began. Cournos does not mention this episode but says merely, "I was the intermediary who brought about a meeting between Gaudier and Pound." [Pound, *Gaudier-Brzeska*, 44-45; Cournos, 260.] Gaudier-Brzeska did a series of pencil sketches of Pound in preparation for the famous cubist bust. Pound purchased several of his works and used Gaudier's profile sketch on his personal stationery. The twenty-four-year-old artist was killed in 1915 while serving with the French army.

Ernest Francisco Fenollosa (1853-1908) was a Massachusetts-born, Harvard-educated economist, best known today as an authority on Oriental art. He spent twenty-eight years in Japan as professor and art curator and did much to awaken Japan to the heritage of its art. He was Imperial Fine Arts Commissioner and for a time manager of the art department of the Imperial Museum in Tokyo. His two-volume *Epochs of Chinese and Japanese Art*

(1911) is a pioneer study of the subject. Upon his death in England, Japan sent a warship for his body and he was buried in the grounds of a temple near Kyoto. For some time his widow had sought someone to edit and publish her husband's manuscripts and, impressed by Pound's poems, she sent all of the papers to him. Already an eager student of Oriental literature and art, Pound examined them with the thrill of the discoverer and set to work on "old Fenollosa's treasures in mss." His first installment of Fenollosa material did appear in the London *Quarterly Review,* not in May, but in the October, 1914 issue, Volume 221, pp. 450-477. Publication of the Fenollosa materials continued to 1959. These documents on Oriental culture influenced Pound's own writing and Yeats' as well. [Brooks, 36-38.]

The volume of Imagist verse appeared in February as Volume I, Number 5 of *The Glebe,* a little magazine conceived by two artists, Samuel Halpert and Man Ray, encouraged by Alfred Kreymborg, and published by Albert and Charles Boni, New York. [Norman, 107-108, 111-113.] Its sixty-three pages contained poetry by Pound, Aldington, Amy Lowell, Ford Madox Hueffer, and others. It was also published in London, as a book.

The New Freewoman (London), edited by Dona Marsden and Harriet Shaw Weaver, became *The Egoist* in January, 1914. Pound had an active interest in its career and tried unsuccessfully to persuade Amy Lowell to become its financial savior. In the February issue began the serialization of Joyce's *A Portrait of the Artist as a Young Man.* [Norman, 133-134.]

Cournos never published his "History of American Painting." After two delays in publication, he decided to revise it but subsequently lost a portion of the manuscript. He has, however, published in periodicals six of the essays intended for the book. [Letter to the editor.]

II, III

THE Untermeyers were touring Italy and, hoping to see Pound, Mr. Untermeyer wrote to determine if Pound was in Rapallo and to ask about local hotels.

V

POUND was just one month shy of his sixteenth birthday when he enrolled as a freshman at the University of Pennsylvania in the fall of 1901, commuting from his father's home in nearby Wyncote. Before long, he met and had long talks with a student named William Carlos Williams, who also had ambitions to write. A few years later another aspiring poet, Hilda Doolittle, entered their circle.

From a list of his undergraduate courses at Pennsylvania, it is easy to see which he considered "irrelevant":

> *1901-1902*—English Composition; English Language and Analysis; Public Speaking; American Colonial History; Solid Geometry; Algebra; Livy; Horace; German Grammar and Reading; Plane Trigonometry; Principles of Government in the United States.
>
> *1902-1903*—English Composition; Cicero; Catullus and Tibullus; Constitutional History of the United States; Logic; Comparative Governments; Foreign Relations of the United States; Ethics; Nineteenth Century English Novelists; The Civil War and Reconstruction; Horace; Propertius and Ovid; Vergil and Lucretius.

Why Pound transferred to Hamilton College is not known, but two possibilities have been mentioned: his poor scholastic showing at Pennsylvania and his father's desire to remove him from a "fast" environment in Philadelphia to a more secluded campus, one near a part of New York state where his kin had once lived. [Norman, 2.]

The new college had something of permanence to give the boy: a knowledge of Anglo-Saxon and a love of Pro-

vençal poetry. Pound's mention of three Hamilton profes-
sors indicates the importance of these two years to him.
First, and pre-eminent, is William Pierce Shepard (1870-
1948), the professor of Romance languages and literatures,
who had been educated at Hamilton and Heidelberg and
was later to write volumes on Provençal literature. Shepard was one of those rare combinations of scholar and
teacher, the sort of teacher who could engender sound and
lasting enthusiasms in his students. In the preface to *The
Spirit of Romance* (1910), Pound expressed his "thanks
. . . to Dr. William Pierce Shepard of Hamilton College,
whose refined and sympathetic scholarship first led me to
some knowledge of French, Italian, Spanish and Provençal." One person in Canto 80 is described as having "a
head built like Bull Shepard's." [80/90.]

Herman Carl George Brandt (1850-1920), born in Germany and brought to America in 1867, was professor of
German.

Rev. Joseph Darlington Ibbotson (1870-1952), was professor of English literature, Anglo-Saxon, and Hebrew.
The students' nickname for him was Bib and a student
yearbook refers to Pound as " 'Bib's' pride." [Norman, 11.]
Pound later said that "the CANTOS started in a talk with
'BIB'." [Norman, 356.] In a letter written in 1959 to Harry
M. Meacham, Pound spoke of the "sonorities due to the
anglo-saxon element in english" and recalled "Bib. Ibbotson's hammering anglo-saxon into me."

How free Pound found himself of irrelevancies can be
seen by a list of the courses he took at Hamilton. Exact
course titles are not available.

   1903-1904—First term: German, French, Italian; Second term: French, Italian, English literature; Third
term: two courses in French, one in Italian.

   1904-1905—First term: Old English; two courses in

French, Spanish; Second term: Old English, Spanish, two courses in French; Third term: German, Old English, French, Provençal, Spanish.

Pound received his Ph. B. from Hamilton in the spring of 1905 and that autumn returned to Pennsylvania to work on his master's degree in Romanics. The majority of his courses were with handsome, dandified Hugo A. Rennert (1858-1927), Professor of Romanic Languages and Literatures, who had just published a celebrated biography of Lope de Vega; but he studied Latin under Assistant Professor Walton B. McDaniel (1871———) and had what he called "an odd sort of post-graduate course" under Professor Cornelius Weygandt (1871-1957). His courses continued the interests developed at Hamilton:

1905-1906—Spanish Drama (Tirso de Molina, Lope de Vega, and Moreto); Spanish literature, "Special Work"; Old French (*Erec und Enid*); Provençal; Italian; and Latin Pro-seminary (according to the University Catalogue, "a special study of Catullus, Martial, or Tacitus").

1906-1907—Early Italian (the Sicilian Poets); Italian (Dante, *La Vita Nuova;* and Boccaccio, *Decamerone*); Old Spanish (*Poema de Fernán González*); Spanish Drama (plays of Miguel Sánchez and Lope de Vega's *La Estrella de Sevilla*); Old Provençal; Old French *(La Chanson de Roland)*.

The University required no master's thesis at the time.

During his second year he held the only Harrison Fellowship granted in Romanics; and with the five hundred dollars which the fellowship provided, Pound made his first independent trip to Europe.

The following autumn he accepted a teaching appointment at Wabash College. He was determined to become a poet, but his thoughts and, perhaps, his affections lay still with the academic world, where he had received the stimulation and knowledge that have shaped and distinguished his poetry. If all had gone well, he might have continued as a teacher, at least for a time; but it would have had to be on the young man's own terms. The Presbyterian mores of Wabash and the constrictions of a small Middle Western town could not, and would not, provide those terms.

A town of 8,500 in central Indiana, Crawfordsville had two distinctions—Wabash College, then in its seventy-fifth year, and General Lew Wallace, who had died just two years earlier. A Chamber of Commerce brochure published in 1929 called Crawfordsville "The Athens of Indiana"; and, in the foreword, Meredith Nicholson, one of the town's celebrities, described it as "the most distinctive and interesting city of its size west of the Alleghenies." His paragraph on the literary gentry mentions Lew Wallace, Mrs. Wallace, Maurice and Will Thompson, and two village poets, Mary Hannah and Caroline Krout.

The post which Pound filled was one of three newly established by the trustees. The Board had voted to shuffle departments and establish three new ones—psychology, history, and Romance languages—and to begin by hiring three young college graduates to man them. [Rader, 7.] Pound's title was "Instructor in Romance Languages" and he constituted the entire department. His approach to his duties as teacher of French and Spanish was unconventional and highly informal. One of his students later recalled that Pound had "an easy approach" to French, but admitted that after a few months he could read French novels with fair facility. [Rader, 8.] Students were soon calling the new instructor "Ezra" and those who could endure Pound's monologues at the soirees in his rooms could hear talk unique to the placid campus.

With his newly acquired continental airs, unconventional dress, and uncommon domestic ways (he cooked strange meals on a chafing dish), Pound was not quite what the trustees had in mind; nor did his practice of cutting chapel exercises endear him. Whether employee and employer could long have coexisted is a matter of some doubt, but Pound's classic indiscretion brought the uneasy alliance to an abrupt end after four months.

On a walk downtown one cold, wintry night in February, 1908, Pound came upon a homeless thespian (variously reported as actress, burlesque performer, and vaudeville girl) and, with generosity more native to Paris than Crawfordsville, offered her shelter for the night. It is said, in one account, that the girl slept in Pound's bed and, in another, that he slept on the floor of his study—though, it may be, he was out of the house altogether. Next morning, while Pound was in his classroom, one of the maiden women who rented him his rooms, coming in to tidy up, was understandably surprised to find the bed so occupied. Her telephone calls to college authorities brought prompt action and Pound's brief professorial career was ended. As the official historian of the College puts it, the trustees "were content to use the occasion to make an arrangement about their contract that encouraged Mr. Pound to shake the dust of a small middle-western Presbyterian college forever from his feet, and content to rejoice in his subsequent triumphs in poetry." [Osborne, 292.]

The facts behind the cryptic last sentence of Pound's first paragraph are not fully known and may never be. The President of the College was George Lewes Mackintosh, 47, a stern Scot, a widower, and a distinguished Presbyterian minister who, it appears, was interested in a young widow of the town. It is altogether possible that, on this fateful night, Pound visited the widow to pass the early part of the evening. There is some basis to believe that she

wrote Mackintosh about the firing. Whatever the circum-
sances, she did not marry the president. [Letters from Mr.
Rader to the editor.]

Just as the University of Pennsylvania subsidized
Pound's earlier trip to Europe, so now did Wabash College, with the severance pay, finance his next. Pound has
mentioned his eighty-dollar balance in *The Cantos* (80/
78), as well as Yusuf (22/103, 104), whom he calls "a damn
good feller" (22/105).

Searchers who have examined denominational files have
failed to locate the early Pound poems reprinted in the
International Sunday School Lesson leaflets. It may be, as
Mr. Donald C. Gallup suggests, that Pound has in mind
the appearance in the *Sunday School Times* (Philadelphia), 1910, of a portion of the "Prologue" which he published in *Canzoni* in mid-1911. [Letter to the editor.]

Pound's "intellexshul biography" first appeared in
Who's Who in America, 1912-1913 (Volume 7) with a
modest ten-line entry. It was expanded in Volume 9 (1916-
1917) to sixteen lines. This was Pound's last real appearance in the work, for Volumes 10 through 21 (1918-1941)
merely refer to the Volume 9 entry. With Volume 22
(1942-1943) the entry disappears altogether. An official of
the publishing firm admits that there is no record of the
reason why the full sketch was dropped as early as 1918.
The policy, he avers, is to drop an entry when an individ-
ual has ceased to have "national reference interest," when
he fails to furnish corrections or new data, or when con-
victed of a felony. Of these three reasons, only the second
could possibly apply in Pound's case—the "disorderly conduct" of failing to answer a biennial data form, in all like-
lihood. The disappearance of Pound's name altogether
in 1942 does suggest war feeling as an unnamed fourth
reason for total exclusion, but his absence in recent
volumes of *Who's Who in America* is probably no source

of grief for either Ezra Pound or Marquis-Who's Who, Inc.

The British *Who's Who* has faithfully and consistently recorded him, beginning with Volume 67 (1915), where Pound described himself as a "vorticist." In the 1919 volume he called himself "poet," and subsequently "poet and constructive critic," "poet and hack writer," and "poet and composer." Pound, whose recreations have been his career, first recorded his "Recreations" for *Who's Who* as "fencing, tennis, searching The Times for evidences of almost incredible stupidity" and then in 1919 altered his entry to read, "The public taste and that of Sir Owen Seaman" —Seaman being an inveterate writer of large letters on small subjects to editors, as well as a versifier for *Punch*.

Pound may or may not have invented the term *imagisme*. Aldington, who says that "Ezra swiped the word from T. E. Hulme," tells how, one day in the spring of 1912 when Pound was examining some unpublished poems written by Aldington and Hilda Doolittle, he announced to the two that they were Imagists. [Aldington, 135.] The genealogy of *vorticism* is more questionable, for it was being used at this time in connection with artists, but used loosely. It is curious to note that the earliest use of *imagist* recorded by the *Oxford English Dictionary* is 1919 (Pound was using *imagiste* in 1912) and the earliest use of *vorticism* is 1915 (Pound was using it in 1914).

Pound's "How to Read" was first published in the *New York Herald Tribune Books* in three installments in January, 1929.

Saying that he has been devoting himself for the past two decades to an "examination of neglected sections of society" is Pound's way of referring to the careful and extensive attention he had been giving to neglected areas of the arts, past and present. In articles, reviews, and books he explored poetry, drama, fiction, art, and music; and he probed deeply into Western culture (the Renaissance, medievalism, classicism, Homer) and deeply into Eastern (Tagore, the Noh drama of Japan, the Chinese poetry of Rihaku, and the Confucian classics).

The mention of Paul Morand, the French novelist, is doubtless a reference to the directionless movement of that compulsive world traveller who admitted, "I shall never be ashamed of my life so long as it continues to possess mobility." [Stansbury, 94.]

By "studies of musicians on the hoof" he refers to his music column written for the *New Age* under the name, "William Atheling," from 1917 to 1921.

Le Testament, Pound's attempt at an opera, was translated into a score with the help of his composer friend, George Antheil. Pound attended to the details of rehearsal and production and sent out invitations to the private hearing at the Salle Pleyel in Paris, June 29, 1926—"Texte de Villon, Musique par Ezra Pound." [Norman, 280-281.]

Personae, The Collected Poems of Ezra Pound was published in New York by Boni and Liveright, 1926, but is not literally "the collected poems."

A Draft of XVI Cantos of Ezra Pound was published in Paris by the Three Mountains Press, 1925, in an elaborate limited edition. The Three Mountains Press was one man and one hand-operated press on the Ile St. Louis, Paris. William Bird, an American journalist, had bought the press and on it he printed, among other titles, the Pound volume, F. M. Ford's *Women and Men,* and Hemingway's *in our time.*

John Rodker in 1928 published *A Draft of the Cantos 17-27 of Ezra Pound* in London in a limited edition of ninety-four copies. Rodker formed The Ovid Press in 1919 and published eight titles (including work by Gaudier-Brzeska, Eliot, Wyndham Lewis, and Pound) until, in 1921, he turned to more lucrative general publishing.

A Draft of XXX Cantos was published in Paris in 1930 by The Hours Press in a limited edition of 212 copies.

The Aquila Press issued its first volume in April, 1929, and expired in July, 1930, before it was able to issue the Cavalcanti volume or the collected prose work. [Ransom, Part One, 4-5.] *Guido Cavalcanti: Rime* was published for Pound in Genoa, 1932, by the Edizioni Marsano.

To a critic, poet, and self-appointed dean of literature such as Pound, activity on literary periodicals was a necessity—an outlet for his developing critical convictions and discoveries. The importance of these "little" magazines with big ideas was considerable, for these were times of literary ferment—Ezra Pound being brewmaster extraordinary. The old established literary magazines continued to ignore the new poetry. What Pound says later in this biographical summary of *Harper's, Century,* and *Scribner's* is fact, not prejudice. The authors of *The Little Magazine* make the same point:

What monthly diet was served by *The Atlantic,* by *Scribner's,* or by *Harper's,* the periodicals which most persons thought of as "good magazines"? They carried from two to five verse tidbits a month, generally of a vapid character, sentimentally designed by such hacksters as Margaret Prescott Montague, Fannie Stearns Davis, Florence Converse, and Margaret Sherwood. Almost completely blind to new talent, *The Atlantic* exhibited during 1912 only one piece of verse by a poet (Amy Lowell) new to the American literary scene. [Hoffman, 34-35.]

The real voice of new forces in poetry was not the venerable *Atlantic* of Boston but Harriet Monroe's *Poetry* of Chicago, which introduced and furthered the work of such poets as Tagore, Richard Aldington, H. D., Vachel Lindsay, George Sterling, Padraic Colum, D. H. Lawrence, Robert Frost, Carl Sandburg, Maxwell Bodenheim, Eunice Tietjens, Wallace Stevens, T. S. Eliot, James Joyce, and Pound. And Pound was, in the early years, responsible for introducing much of this new poetry.

The Little Review (Chicago; New York; Paris, 1914-1929) had three phases of development, according to Hoffman's *The Little Magazine,* and the second period, April 1917-1921, was its "Ezra Pound period," one in which he helped to enlarge its service to modern letters by securing for it the work of Yeats, Hart Crane, Aldington, Eliot, John Rodker, Wyndham Lewis, and others. From 1918 to 1920, the magazine serialized a substantial portion of Joyce's *Ulysses.*

Pound was largely responsible for rechristening *The New Freewoman* (London) as *The Egoist, an Individualist Review* (1914-1919) and had a hand in the serialization of Joyce's *A Portrait of the Artist as a Young Man.*

The Dial (New York, 1920-1929) opened its pages to the lively and probing criticism of Pound, Eliot, Kenneth Burke, and Yvor Winters, and had a first of equal importance: the first printing in America of Eliot's *The Waste Land.*

Pound's own magazine, *The Exile* (Dijon; Chicago; New York, 1927-1928) survived for only four issues but, again, Pound was instrumental in publishing another modern classic—Yeats' "Sailing to Byzantium."

Pound continues to document what clearly is to him an important claim to fame—his position in the forefront of literary developments. *Cathay* (London, 1915) was a thirty-two page pamphlet of translations of Chinese poetry, the first use of the Fenollosa manuscripts outside periodicals. His claim of primacy in discovering Tagore is valid. His first article, "Tagore's Poems," in the December, 1912 issue of *Poetry,* was followed by another in early 1913 in the *Fortnightly Review,* and a third in late 1913 in *The New Freewoman.* Tagore's *Gitanjali* was published in 1913. Pound not only called attention to Tagore in critical writings but also introduced his poetry to America by forwarding poems for publication in *Poetry*. Indeed, Harriet Monroe invited Tagore to Chicago, while he was in the United States, with interesting results. [See Hay, 442-444.] Pound's early essays on Joyce and Lewis appeared in *The Egoist* in January and June, 1914. His article on Joyce and Flaubert was indeed an early one on the subject: "James Joyce et Pécuchet," *Mercure de France*, Volume 156, pages 307-320 (June, 1922).

He had first heard of the struggling Joyce through Yeats and, not one to let a man of promise languish, he had written the despairing young man on December 15, 1913. Did Joyce have any work on hand? He had connections, Pound said, with two struggling English magazines and two more prosperous American ones, Mencken's *Smart Set* and Monroe's *Poetry*. Before Joyce could reply, Pound wrote again, asking the use of one of Joyce's poems in *Des Imagistes*—and offering to pay. "Thus encouraged," Joyce's biographer says, "Joyce made final revisions on the first chapter of *A Portrait of the Artist as a Young Man*, and sent it, along with *Dubliners*, to Pound in mid-January [1914]." [Ellman, 361.] With help from Yeats, Pound was able to get a grant for Joyce of £100 from the Civil List in 1915; Pound forwarded an anonymously given £25 in mid-year; and Pound engineered a £2-a-week grant for thirteen weeks from the Society of Authors—a grant later renewed for three months more. [Ellman, 419.] Pound's being the generation's most amazing literary prospector was not all due to merely lucky strikes.

Pound's early article on Eliot, a review of his first book, *Prufrock and Other Observations*, appeared in *Poetry*, August, 1917. Eliot's verse appeared first in book form in Pound's *Catholic Anthology: 1914-1915* (London, 1915). The article by Edmund Wilson to which Pound refers is doubtless "T. S. Eliot," *New Republic*, Volume 60, pages

341-349 (November 13, 1929)—a detailed and favorable estimate of Eliot as poet and critic. However, Wilson had written on Eliot much earlier—a review of *The Waste Land* in *The Dial,* December, 1922, in less favorable terms.

At the bottom of the last page of Letter V, in Untermeyer's hand, is the following notation:

Tell Harcourt about booklet on "How to Read, or Why" based on 3 articles in Herald Tribune "Books" Jan. 13. 20 27. Vol 5 = No. 17-18-19) Also The International Anthology. on which E. P. will collaborate with LU

Pound had hope that Untermeyer, after his Rapallo visit, could persuade his publisher, Harcourt, Brace and Company, to issue the "How to Read" essays in book form. The firm declined but a London edition appeared in 1931. Shortly thereafter, Bruce Humphries of Boston imported and distributed a French edition. The other project is more interesting, though it failed. During the visit, Pound proposed that Untermeyer help him to compile an "International Anthology," which would represent and display the work of *avant garde* poets in the Western world. As he conceived the volume, they would seek out new and virtually unpublished poets of worth to supplement the work of already known modern poets— Pound to cover Italy, France, and England; Untermeyer to be responsible for Germany and America. The two drew up a prospectus and, upon his return to New York, Untermeyer sought to interest several publishers in the book. None were interested, possibly, in part, because of Pound's reputation for intransigeance with publishers.

By arrangement of Mr. Pound with Mr. Donald Hall, advisory editor of the *Paris Review,* this biographical summary appeared in No. 28 of the *Review* (Summer-Fall, 1962, issue). The date of the summary is given in the *Paris Review* as 1932 (which indeed is the date ascribed to it in

Mr. Untermeyer's notation), though both internal evidence and Mr. Untermeyer's reflection on the point confirm 1930 as the true date.

VI

POUND speaks as a translator of Heine, for he had published versions of several of Heine's poems in *Personae* in 1909. [Demetz, 286 and *passim*.] Untermeyer had translated and published a selection of *Poems of Heinrich Heine* in 1917 and he had in mind, meanwhile, a more complete edition and a biography of the poet. This he published in 1937 in two volumes as *Heinrich Heine, Paradox and Poet*. "Diese Damen," the opening section of "Yolanda and Marie," does appear in the two-volume work, and the translation is as representative of Untermeyer as Pound's is of him:

> Both of them know how to honor
>   Poets; they do not discuss
> Art. Instead, they give me luncheon,
>   Me and my great genius.
>
> Ah! The soup was most auspicious,
>   And the wine increased the mood;
> The roast chicken was delicious,
>   And the larded hare was good.
>
> And the Muse? We dined upon her,
>   Full to tears, and loath to part;
> And I thanked them for the honor
>   That they showed me and my art.

Pound's comments on parodies refer to the section of Untermeyer's *Collected Parodies* (1926) called "Including Horace"—Horatian subject and manner as they might be rendered by Browning, Whitman, and other poets. (*Including Horace* had been published separately in 1919.)

Mark Van Doren had chosen fifty-three of Heine's poems for his *An Anthology of World Poetry* (1928)—including one translation by Pound.

VIII

THIS letter is written, in ink, on the reverse of a printed order form of the London publisher, A. & C. Black, Ltd., publisher of the British *Who's Who*. On the form, Pound has placed an X opposite this title: "The Book of Saints. A Dictionary of Servants of God canonised by the Catholic Church. . . A complete record of the saints with brief biographies in the style of 'Who's Who.' "

During his 1929-30 trip to Europe, Untermeyer had been captivated by the miniature donkeys of Sicily and had purchased two of them for his farm in the Adirondacks. He later turned them to literary use in *The Donkey of God* (1932). [See Untermeyer, 343 ff.]

IX

DURING 1931 Untermeyer was at work on a new anthology, which Harcourt, Brace and Company published in 1932 under the title, *The Book of Living Verse*. The English edition was published the following year by W. Collins Sons and Company as *The Albatross Book of Living Verse*. Untermeyer had written Pound for advice and permission, and in this letter Pound says that the formal arrangements will have to be made through Boni and Liveright, who had published American editions of his poetry in the twenties. Untermeyer's list of suggested poems has riled Pound, who feels that such choices misrepresent him.

The answer lies in the nature of this new anthology. The rationale, suggested in the title, is made explicit in the preface: "The selections in this volume are living poetry in the sense that they have persisted in spite of changing times and shifting tastes." In the instance of recent poems, where judgment is clearly more precarious, the editor says that his selections, he hopes, will "possess the quality which implies permanence." The volume was a brave editorial enterprise—to select poems, both English and American, from the thirteenth century to the present, which have had, or are likely to have, an imperishable popular appeal. Choices from the work of the more esoteric contemporary poets would have to be intelligent guesses. Inevitably, they would be choices not necessarily representative of the total work of a poet and not necessarily the favorite of the critic or knowledgeable reader. Inevitably, Pound would bristle about such an undertaking, as he does in this letter—but he does not withdraw candidacy.

———

There is a tenth letter, dated Rapallo, September 24, 1933, which may not now be published. By this time, Untermeyer's *Book of Living Verse* had been published and, looking over a copy, Pound scorned it in sharp and vigorous terms.

Pound did not scorn anthologies as such. He was an anthologist himself, he had assisted in a new edition of *Modern American Poetry* (Letter V), and he and Untermeyer had talked of collaborating. The answer doubtless lies in the, in this instance, divergent purposes of the two men, for in October Pound's newest anthology appeared. His title was *Active Anthology* and in a prefatory note he explained that he was interested in "writers . . . in whose verse a development appears or in some case we may say 'still appears' to be taking place." It is difficult to imagine two anthologies more antithetical in purpose and philosophy. Or—might it be?—Pound could not abide the thought that any of his poems were becoming household favorites.

WORKS CITED

John Edwards' *A Preliminary Checklist of the Writings of Ezra Pound, Especially his Contributions to Periodicals* (New Haven, Conn.: Kirgo-Books, 1953) is a valuable source of bibliographical information, but I have not cited this work, inasmuch as Donald C. Gallup's more complete bibliography of Ezra Pound will shortly be published.

Aldington, Richard. *Life for Life's Sake* (New York: The Viking Press, 1941).

Brooks, Van Wyck. *Fenollosa and His Circle, with Other Essays in Biography* (New York: Dutton, 1962).

Cournos, John. *Autobiography* (New York: G. P. Putnam's Sons, 1935).

Demetz, Peter. "Ezra Pound's German Studies." *Germanic Review*, XXXI (December, 1956), 279-292.

Ellman, Richard. *James Joyce* (New York: Oxford University Press, 1959).

Hay, Stephen N. "Rabindranath Tagore in America." *American Quarterly*, XIV (Fall, 1962), 439-463.

Hoffman, Frederick J., Charles Allen, and Carolyn F. Ulrich. *The Little Magazine, A History and a Bibliography* (Princeton, N.J.: Princeton University Press, 1947).

Monroe, Harriet. *A Poet's Life: Seventy Years in a Changing World* (New York: The Macmillan Company, 1938).

Norman, Charles. *Ezra Pound* (New York: The Macmillan Company, 1960).

Osborne, James Insley, and Theodore Gregory Gronert. *Wabash College, The First Hundred Years, 1832-1932* (Crawfordsville, Ind.: R. E. Banta, 1932).

Paige, D. D., ed. *The Letters of Ezra Pound* (New York: Harcourt, Brace, and World, 1950).

Pound, Ezra. *The Cantos* (New York: New Directions, 1948). References to passages are given with two numerals, the first being the canto number and the second the page number of this edition.

Pound, Ezra. *Gaudier-Brzeska, A Memoir* (New York: New Directions, 1960). First published, 1916.

Rader, James E. "Ship in the Night," *The Bachelor* (student publication of Wabash College, Crawfordsville, Ind.), Vol. 50, No. 26, Section 2 (May 9, 1958), pp. 7-10—a summary of Pound's career at Wabash. References are to this article. Pound's stay at Wabash is the subject of another article by Rader: "A Pound of Flesh," *Wabash College Review,* Vol. 6, No. 1 (Spring, 1959), pp. 5-10.

Ransom, Will. *Selective Check Lists of Press Books* (New York: P. C. Duschnes, 1945-50; published in twelve parts).

Rosenthal, Macha L. *The Modern Poets, A Critical Introduction* (New York: Oxford University Press, 1960).

Stansbury, Milton H. *French Novelists of Today* (Philadelphia: University of Pennsylvania Press, 1935).

Untermeyer, Louis. *From Another World: The Autobiography of Louis Untermeyer* (New York: Harcourt, Brace, and World, 1939).